THE SEA AND THE TOWER

GEORGE MACKAY BROWN

THE SEA AND THE TOWER

Illustrations by

Erlend Brown

BAYEUX

© George Mackay Brown 1994
Illustrations © Erlend Brown 1994

First published in 1994
by Bayeux Arts Incorporated,
Suite 240, 4411 Sixteenth Avenue, N.W.,
Calgary, Alberta, Canada T3B 0M3

Canadian Cataloguing in Publication Data
Brown, George Mackay.
The sea and the tower

Poems
ISBN 1-896209-00-9

1. Trojan War – Poetry. 1. Title.
PR6052.R59S4 1994   823'.914   CX94-910407-8

Printed and bound in Canada at
Friesen Printers, Altona, Manitoba

Contents

To the Fishermen and Sailors of Orkney

THE SEA AND THE TOWER

BY

GEORGE MACKAY BROWN

Village Elders Consult a Sea-chart

Village Elders Consult a Sea-chart

Women and girls
Don't come to this door any night this week.

Provision is made for you, written and sealed.

See to the loom and the hearth,
See to grapes, fleeces, honeycombs.
Be early at the spring with your jars.

If wife or widow or girl
Tilts ear to this door
Her ear will sing with a fist, no cry of welcome!
Have a care, Xanthe. Even you.

Are other shores than this.
A man is none the worse
Of one voyage
Further than the fishing grounds. There should be
One far-fetched golden thread
Through the pitiful rags of age.

You whose business is bread baking,
We sail east to free a queen
From a black tower. All women
Will toss like roses in the wind of that dawn.
A skipper is instructing us
In foreign words.
We are learning to handle a larger spread of sail.

If any soldier should die
Of fever or wounds or a sea greenness,
Make suitable intercession
For a young ghost.
Pour wine, light a lamp in a temple niche.

The Deepening Ocean

The Deepening Ocean

That waste and confusion of sevens, the sea

In the pool, there children stoop
Upon starfish and limpet

At the inshore, on rocks
A cormorant visits, a boy's slack line
Tautens, ends in a twist of silver

Further out, the station for soundings,
For spreading of nets.
<u>Over there</u>! Gulls are jostling
Like miners at a new shaft: the shoal

There is a distance, a depth
Where those who watch from shore
Eyes keener than knives at oystershells
Cannot prise open
Curves of sea and sky, the horizon

Vaster still, the whale-acre, the skipper
Alone with a star,
The merchant asleep under awning,
Bill of lading and gold pieces
Fast sewn into tunic,
Bales and winecasks below, waxed against spume

Last, the open perilous
Road of the venturers, where a sudden
Wheel of tempest
May overset the delicate dance of our sea horse.
Yet even so, to such a bourne -
Ruin or harvesting -
The least bondman must lead his age

Tradesman

Tradesman

Me, I have no love for ship or voyage.
I would be planing now
At the workbench, or making dovetails
To be tables and benches
For such as unlock a new echoing house.

'At the end of the voyage,' they wheedled
'A purse crammed with coins.'
To win war bounty I toil on a seabench.

By no small gift of pegs or door-latch
Do they dimple at me, the girls.
The plainest turn from the plane-man.
A pot of foreign gold should get me a good wife.

If I had Xanthe for sweetheart
Like that fool at the helm
No chest of silver or sea-pearls
Would have reft me from the shore.
And it is quite possible
Never more will he set eyes on his Xanthe.

I know this, the jars of loot
Will not be handed to us
When we wade with seabright legs to the tower.
The way to the treasure
Is through wounds, fire, fracturings,
And he who offers wounds
Must expect a bruise or a graze or worse.

As for me, I would as soon
Wind in the arms of the war-maidens

Than go back to that shore of flower-cold faces.

The Resignation of Seamen

The Resignation of Seamen

That there must be voyages
That a man should labour at oar
Then put a hungry hand
Among twelve hands at the common fish-pot

That a score of beards
Be crusted from the same great comber
And forty eyes or more
Take wrinkles from sun-fire
That there be, after an upturned wine jar
Fury, flung fists, the cold ashes of sleep

(I throw dice with Hylas at the gameboard)

That the hollow bird, the ship
Furl near a city
Of wheels, horses, trumpets, swords, treasure

That certain ghosts troop
From riven heart-root to riverbank

Where the ferryman bites upon fee
Then sets them without order
On viewless thwarts
In a hull clinkered with shadows,
Then casts off upon the death flood

Thus and thus fate must take us
But that this venturer or that
Singly might wend home
To tall sons and a gray bitter
Baker of fish and bread
And there beg acceptance
And light a lamp frequently to the gods of ocean and war

Night at Sea

Night at Sea

Sunset, the trodden garlands, gules and gold!
Apollo, charioteer
Looses the long necks now for dew and herbage.
Follow him! Turn and follow.
Westward the spirit yearneth always.

We urge our ship another way
Against the starwheel.
Night. A spindrifting glimmer.
The boy hangs a lantern at the mast.

Where now the golden bridle, the hooves and axle?

Above, below, the strict compulsion,
The Ox, the Crab, the Scales, the Lion,

Bearer-of-water, the Twins, the Virgin, the Ram,
Scorpion, Archer, Capricorn, Fish.
None pits his fate against the star scroll.

We have signed the parchment, firm we are set
To greet the golden horseman.
Frail seahorse, we spur it
Through sleep and the faces that drift in sleep.
We will welcome the aureate sky-team
When once more silently
It breaks the line of Asia to roses and ingots.

Old voices: <u>Apples of youth, another shore</u>!
<u>Westward the tribes are bidden</u>.
<u>Not here among witherings,</u>
<u>Heart-bruisings, urns, is our bourne</u>.
The helmsman takes the sun on his forehead.
We must mell with foreign horses under a tower.

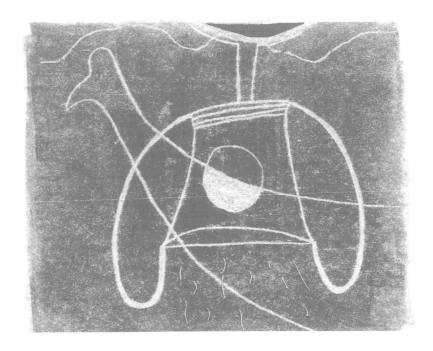

Thirst

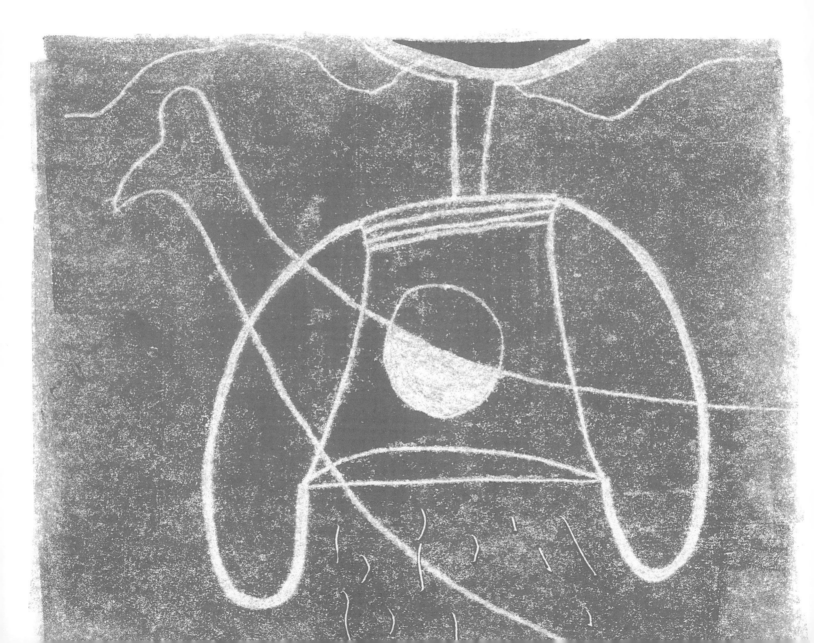

Thirst

In the days without rain, oarsmen sang
The virtue of various juices.

As: 'I remember shaking
Silver drops from my coat. I cursed
That hill-torn cloud.'

Another: 'Zoe's grapes are gathered
In tarnish of autumn,
Then trodden with rhythmic feet.
All winter about the vat
The drunken feet, throng after throng.'

I think of Xanthe at the stream, with jars.

Milk of cow and goat was discussed,
The Olympian cup
Ganymede bears to the deathless mouths.
Our ship-boy lay at the scuppers
As one who sipped at a cold high source.
And the beachcomber,
'I have drunk at a seabird's throat.'

None mentioned the drench, spume, salt siftings.
Under and around us
Rose the fountains, brimming, where crayfish
And dolphins drink, where the kerulos
Over the wave's flower wings and sips.
None praised the tilting brim of ocean.

'Yet once' said the forester, 'when
I was dry with burning of leaves
I put a stone in my mouth.
My cheek hollowed like a drained peach.'

Rain

Rain

Water rotted in the casks,
A green mantle over dregs.
Worms crept out of stave joints
Worms idled in the green slime.

Islanders, ironbrows, stood at a shore
Guarding ancestors' wells.
Hags shrieked, their knees seawashed.
The skipper flashed a silver coin.
No bargaining! Eyrie to ebbmark

Fruitless for seafarers the fresh streams flowed.

We sailed east. Keel and oars
Tore the blue silk.
The sky blue curves, hot clay out of a kiln.

Noon over our labouring shoulders
Splashed the molten gold.

The fisherman, 'I heard at sunrise
The seamew that calls for rain...'
The bailers looked longingly
Into the bailing pans
Throwing salt syllables from the scoops
Into the huge monotony of ocean.

A drop hit the helmsman's knuckle.
He tongued it. <u>Dew</u>!
From a dark cloud the honey was everywhere.
Four held a slack sail
By the four corners. Hair streamed.
Mouths gaped. Their faces
Were like the faces of blest spirits.

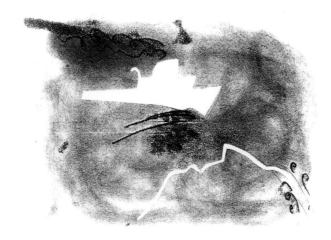

Fog

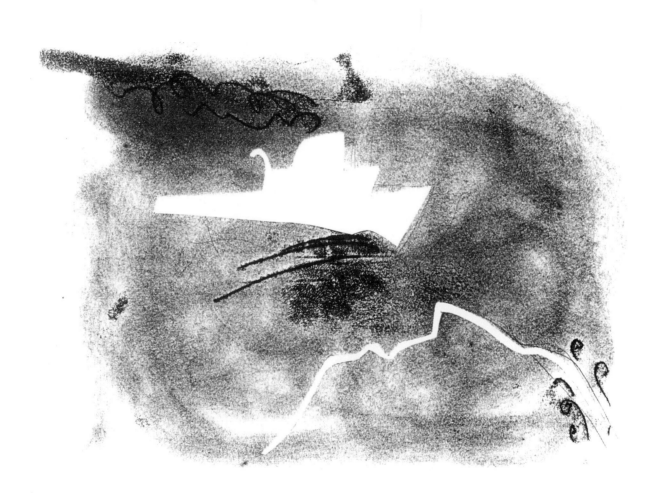

Fog

In a fog we lingered, lapsed
And loitered, five days
In a blind fog, the sun a ghost.

The helmsman made his ear a conch
Seeking shore breakers.

The pure eye of the ship boy
Was wrapped with those gray clouts.
Dolphins surged past, whether
East or north or south or west
Whale-knowledge only.
No dolphin to take the ship by the hand.
The beards were dense with seed pearls.

Fell on me, friend of Xanthe
(Does she kneel beside the springs?)
A dream at noon. Two seamen
Threw dice on the thwart. One
Tapped the hollow water-keg.
My silvered eyes beheld a ghost ship.

The ship smoked skywards
From a tall tube.
A bronze ship it was, it rang!
The heart of the ship
Thudded, thudded. It smoked, stank.

A sailor with one long eye-stalk
Hailed, 'Are you for Ilium
With a cargo of white birds?'
We rocked in the wash of the ship.

I woke. Dice rattled. The boy was weeping.

There Was A Ship

There Was A Ship

'There was a ship.' Needeth be said no more,
'There was a ship.'
From bridefeast feet will draw
To the spell, thus, 'There was a ship.'
A sea mouth. One listener, lingering, compelled.

A ship. All seekings, urges, speculations
By men or gods crafted
Are stamped with one image: <u>ship</u>

Birth-keel, the clean curves of youth,
The proud horizon-trampler,
Come too soon to rust and warpage.
Mariner calleth on the dark bird for enfoldment.

'There was a ship', quoth he.

This globe of rivers, orchards, cities
A keel upon chaos set,
Nor can knowledge oracular
Nor wisdom spun on the sweet looms of thought
Chart the voyage, whether
End will be haven, or rock, or fire gnawing at hull and thwart.

Make a true bill of lading. Be thy hold stored
With wine-jars, corn-jars, oil-jars
Sun-nurtured, sealed with wax of the sun,
A considered excess of harvest
For exchange of foreign coinage -
No cargo of black edges
To trade for a queen no better than a fishwife.

<u>There was a ship</u>. Let the skipper
Bright-bearded, tread the wharf with a grave merchant.

Visitant

Visitant

The bird made no response from the prow,
Then with bird syllables responded.

Where have you come from, bird?
Have you come to tell us
How it is with the shifting armies?
Does the stone wait for us
That we alone can wrench from the wall,
The keystone of the tower?
The bird tilts a wise eye at our toil.

Have you come from the little island
Where neither fame was nor wealth?
The bird folds wings upon silence.

How is it with Xanthe at the well?

I hope she has not sold our goat
To go like a butterfly to the fair at Kos.
We think of Helen sometimes
Set in rags among Trojan ladies.

Tell Xanthe, with much oar-toil
And with eating cheese like wedges of wood
And with squinnying on the seachart
And with a nor'east wind
That has scoured the hull nine days...
She should weave a small cage for you.

The bird shrieked from the mast.
All at once, the bird
Bade them 'return!' or 'sail on!'
With wing-claps of valediction
The messenger was in and out of a new wave.

The Helmsman's Dream of the Elements

The Helmsman's Dream of the Elements

Then, it seemed, after Chronos and Saturn
Stood four handmaids about the throne.
'Be thou, the first, mantled in blue. Utter
Rain and wind and snow. Wear
The steepled crown of stars.
Span the blue, sweetest of girls,
A thread upon the lips of all living.'

On the green coat of one sister is sown
A flock of sheep,
Villages, a towered city with seven gates,
A forest, a mountain,
Roses, eagles, temples, goats, a cornfield.

This is whose unquiet house we wander
Is Xanthe at the well-head,
Xanthe with her pitcher and pegged linen.
She is the woman raging
At a fisherman home from the winebench late.
She has ship and dolphin sewn on her coat.

The helmsman nodded thrice
In the first smoulders of sunrise.

He gave the steering-oar to the first watch.

The three sisters before his proper sleep
Scattered their gifts,
Crust and crabclaw, a frail
Bede-broken breath at the lips.

He dreamed again - Xanthe upsetting her lamp
Beside her loom -
A tower wrapped in a long red coat.

Watchman: Night Sea

Watchman: Night Sea

Waves came on, hooded. They streamed, unbodied
From, it seemed, sundered deaths,
Like souls in surge from a sacked city.

Each seemed to bear, half hid, an image
Of what, living, it most had affected.
One bore a gray falcon at fist.
One fingered careful coins, all tarnish.

One cherished a bronze comb
Wherewith some woman
Still, it might be, stretched yellow hair at a lamp.
One reeled under a broken shield -
All with bitterest lamentation paused and passed.

One flung (hooded) a harp at the hull.

I charted the trek of those thousands
And pitied somewhat their pain.
I considered at last
How time might take their tattered keenings
Into one web of dark pure threnody
(My ear assoiled
From snores and scattered night-sighs under the thwarts.)

Only the honey of the boy's sleep
Made true response to the wailing between two shores.

The harp had drenched me, beard to shinbone.
There soon, the loom of light
Would clothe me in a silver sea-smock.
A sailor woke. He shivered. He spat.
His face flushed ... Well went the keel
On a hundred labouring shoulders.